HSK真题集解析

Analyses of
HSK Official Examination Papers

2014版

3级

华语教学出版社
SINOLINGUA

First Edition 2014

ISBN 978-7-5138-0724-1

Published by Sinolingua Co., Ltd
24 Baiwanzhuang Road, Beijing 100037, China
Tel: (86)10-68320585, 68997826
Fax: (86)10-68997826, 68326333
http://www.sinolingua.com.cn
E-mail: hyjx@sinolingua.com.cn
Facebook: www.facebook.com/sinolingua
Printed by Beijing Jinghua hucais Printing Co., Ltd.

Printed in the People's Republic of China

Preface

The HSK is a national level standard test, which is tailored to test the proficiency of non-native Chinese speakers. Since the revision of the HSK test in 2009, it has become much more adaptable to the spread of the Chinese language worldwide.

Students can acquaint themselves with the material as well as its style by doing the exercises from the HSK Official Examination Papers. These papers can not only test students' levels of Chinese, but also help them to master commonly used vocabulary and grammatical points that they may confuse by offering them the chance to learn and do these exercises repeatedly. In order to help HSK examinees prepare for the test more effectively and systematically, this book offers an explanation for each exercise in the HSK Official Examination Papers (2014 edition) in detail; it also has a focus on the explanation of vocabulary and grammatical points that are easily misused so as to help students avoid misunderstandings in the Chinese language. This book can guide students to pass the HSK test more easily.

The book has many distinctive features:

Scientific: The book is compiled based on the HSK syllabus and offers detailed analysis of the vocabulary and grammatical points in the HSK Official Examination Papers (2014 edition), which can help students to better understand the test features and master the exercises.

Authoritative: The book is written by instructors who are engaged in teaching Chinese and have been offering instruction on the HSK test to international students for many years. Since the compilers are familiar with each HSK test point, this book can aid teachers and students in preparing for the test more effectively.

Self-learning: This book intends to keep the language simple to explain each difficult point of the exercise in detail. This book is not only conducive for teachers explaining these language points, but also for students learning by themselves. Self-learning can further enhance students' ability to imagine, conjecture, respond and comprehend Chinese language, and can also improve their logical thinking, analyzing, summarizing competence and the ability to grasp the framework of vocabulary words. This book can act as a teaching plan for teachers as well as a tool for students learning Chinese.

We expect teachers, HSK examinees and other readers to share their insights with us. You can contact us via email hyjx@sinolingua.com.cn or via micro blog http://weibo.com//sinolinguavip.

The Compilers

May, 2014

《HSK 真题集解析（2014 版）》编委会

策划：全球 HSK 策划大队

顾问：解　惜

编委：（按姓氏笔画顺序排列）

[泰] นางปุณยพัทธ์ โถชาลี（冯丽颖）　史文华　曲玉彬

孙中华　陈　瑜　李改如　贾　昉　章辉辉　解　惜

校对：梁　杉

目　录

H31221 卷答案解析……1

一、听力 Listening Section……1
二、阅读 Reading Section……6
三、写作 Writing Section……10

H31222 卷答案解析……12

一、听力 Listening Section……12
二、阅读 Reading Section……17
三、写作 Writing Section……21

H31223 卷答案解析……23

一、听力 Listening Section……24
二、阅读 Reading Section……28
三、写作 Writing Section……33

H31224 卷答案解析……35

一、听力 Listening Section……35
二、阅读 Reading Section……39
三、写作 Writing Section……43

H31225 卷答案解析……45

一、听力 Listening Section……45
二、阅读 Reading Section……49
三、写作 Writing Section……53

H31221 卷答案解析

一、听力 Listening Section

第一部分 Part One

Keys to Questions 1—5: A C E F B

1. A

It can be deduced from 高 that the question must be related to one's height and features. A shows a girl measuring her height with a ruler, so it is the correct answer.

2. C

行李箱 is mentioned in the recording. We may think B and C are both correct as they are related to 箱. But if we continue to listen, 太小了 and 放不进去 in the recording show that C is the correct picture which contains a piece of luggage that cannot be closed.

3. E

考试 and 复习 are mentioned in the recording, and these words are related to reading and study. So E is the correct answer.

4. F

In the recording, the man asked 这两个人是谁. Only in Picture F are there two people.

5. B

箱子 is mentioned in the recording again. 碗 and 筷子 mentioned in the recording are only meant to confuse the listener. The correct answer is B, which is also the only option left.

Keys to Questions 6—10: D A B E C

6. D

The first word 妈 in the recording shows D is the correct answer to the exercise, which can be further confirmed as 骑 is mentioned twice in the recording. In Picture D, there is a mother and a son who is learning to ride a bike.

7. A

After hearing 帽子, you can find the answer. Only pictures A and D contain a person with a hat. But choice D has been chosen, so A is the correct answer.

8. B

The key word here is 相机, although it appears only once. Words like 换 and 没换 in the recording may mislead you into believing A is the correct answer, but A has been chosen, so we can choose B directly. It is very important to catch the key words.

9. E

It is not easy to choose the correct answer to the exercise. Since there is no picture showing a scene of playing in the snow, it seems that no picture matches with 雪越来越大 and 再玩儿一会儿 in the recording. However, in Picture E, a girl is holding an umbrella to shelter herself from the rain or snow. If we look at the picture more carefully, we can see the girl is wearing a scarf. So it can be deduced that this picture is related to a freezing and snowy day.

10. C

The key to the exercise is to spot the laptop in Picture C. 上网 in the first sentence of the recording shows that a laptop should be included in the picture. So C is the correct answer.

第二部分 Part Two

11. ✓

一千多块 is mentioned in the recording. Based on this figure, this statement can be confirmed as true.

12. ×

Special attention should be paid to the change of concepts when we do this exercise. In the recording, it says that the book introduces 节日 so as to acquaint children with 文化 from different countries. Despite that 音乐 is a part of 文化, this recording only touches upon 节日文化. So this statement is false.

13. ×

Generally speaking, if the statement contains the words expressing absolute senses like 必须, 一定, it is highly likely to be false. Based on the key points 自己多想办法 and 不能总是让别人 in the recording, it can be deduced that the statement and the recording are contrary in meaning.

14. ✓

Focus should be put on synonyms in this exercise. 那个地方的茶很有名 in the statement means the same as 那里的茶非常有名 in the recording.

15. ✓

It is not difficult to find the correct answer. Although there are a lot of descriptions of where 校长 is standing, the focus remains on 校长. 他很年轻 in the latter part fits in with the statement 校长很年轻, so the statement is consistent with the recording.

16. ×

Eggs, bread, milk and fruit juice are mentioned but apples are not, so the statement is false.

17. ×

It is unlikely that 他们正在看电影. Expressions like 对不起, 突然有事儿 and 下星期再一起去 in the recording show that they are not watching a movie together now.

18. ✓

There is a lot of information in the former part of the recording. However, you won't find the statement 王阿姨会打篮球 correct until you hear the final sentence 但她的篮球打得非常好.

19. ×

手表不见了 is mentioned in the recording, and 这让他很难过 in the latter part shows that the speaker hasn't found his watch. So the statement 他找到手表了 is obviously false.

20. ✓

The key information often comes after the clause introduced by 除了. 考试时只能用铅笔 is mentioned after the first clause, which shows that pencils are needed when you take the exam. So the statement 考试要带铅笔 fits in line with the recording.

第三部分 Part Three

21. A

The key to this exercise is to hear and recognize the word 电梯. We can also find the answer from a different approach. If the words 教室 and 办公室 that are easily memorized and commonly used are not mentioned in the recording, A will be the correct answer.

22. A

这是我大学同学 in the recording shows that the person the woman is introducing is her 同学.

23. C

Synonyms are tested in the exercise again. In the recording, you will hear 发现自己没带钱包, which has the same meaning as 忘拿钱包了 in the statement. So C is the correct answer.

1

24. C

After hearing the recording, you will know the man is going to 图书馆, but he doesn't know how to get there. So C is the correct answer.

25. C

累 is mentioned in the recording. We can start by imagining the feeling of being tired, and when being tired, a rest will be well-warranted. In the recording, though the man asks the woman if she would like some water to drink, what the woman wants is 休息. So C is the correct answer.

26. B

The key word 听 in the recording shows that it has nothing to do with 写, so C should be ruled out first. If the woman 不懂汉语, she won't say the story is 很有意思. So B is the correct answer because it shows that the female speaker thinks the story is good.

27. B

In the recording, the female speaker expresses her surprise and then asks the man why his room is so clean. So it can be deduced that the cleanliness is unusual and is a bit surprising. This statement has nothing to do with 女儿, so A should be ruled out first. And apparently, C is incorrect, because the reason why the boy cleaned his dormitory is that his mother will visit him. So B is the correct answer.

28. B

In the recording, 要上飞机了 demonstrates that the speakers are waiting for their plane at 机场. So B is the correct answer.

29. C

In the recording, the woman asks if she has gained weight. A man should never tell a lady that she becomes fat because of common decency. Therefore, the man says 没变化 to the lady, which sounds a polite response. So C is the correct answer.

30. B

Common sense won't help you to find the answer to the exercise, so you should listen to the recording carefully. Since 邻居 appears twice in the recording while 弟弟 and 奶奶 are never mentioned, B can be confirmed as the correct answer.

第四部分　Part Four

31. B

The recording introduces the topic at the beginning. When asked what she thinks of the trousers, the woman replies 不错. 不错 should be the focus when you listen. This reply is sensible, since no one is willing to buy something 普通. In addition, comparisons between other trousers are never made in the dialogue.

32. C

In the recording, the old 桌子 is mentioned first, then the speakers suggest 桌子和椅子 be changed. Even if you don't catch the word 椅子, 盘子 and 自行车 from the choices are never mentioned in the recording, so these choices can be ruled out, and you can choose C.

33. C

Two clues can help you get the correct answer of 踢足球. Among the choices, the other two activities won't be influenced if the weather changes, because these activities can be done indoors. Meanwhile, the verb 踢 is mentioned twice, so C is the correct answer.

34. A

This exercise is not easy because 离开 is mentioned only once, and if we want to know if the man will leave, we must figure out the implication of the key words 要回去, 说再见 , 有机会见面 and 去我们那儿玩儿 in the context. Listening again, you will find 真不想现在就离开北京 in the recording shows the answer.

35. A

The key to the exercise is to hear the first question 累了吧 and its answer 是 clearly. 休息 in the third sentence can further confirm that the woman is tired. So A is the correct answer.

36. B

The recording focuses on the good relations between the man and Xiao Wang in the photo. The first sentence 这张照片上 ... shows B is the correct answer; as well, A and C are never mentioned.

37. B

Several food names and the verbs 买 and 要 used for shopping appear in the recording. In addition, the key information 客人 shows that the man will buy something to treat the guest(s). So B is the correct answer which shows the man is going to do some shopping.

38. A

三层, 走楼梯, 电梯 and 疼 in the dialogue between the man and the woman share links with 脚. So A is the correct answer.

39. B

It is easy to choose A because having something to eat seems to be discussed in the recording. But upon listening further, you will find the reason why the woman doesn't want to eat has nothing to do with 饿了 or not, but that she 发烧, which is related to 生病.

40. A

The recording may flummox you because the two location words 东 and 西 are often related to 地图. In the recording, the sun is mentioned but the moon is not, so B can be ruled out first. If you continue to listen, weather related words like 下雨, 晴天, 夏天 are mentioned further, so C 地图 can be ruled out as well.

二、阅读 Reading Section

第一部分 Part One

Keys to Questions 41—45: B D C F A

Tips: While doing this type of matching exercise, the key is to find the appropriate words or phrases through the similarities, relevance or connections. The exercises here are designed based on starting from the easiest and moving to the hardest.

41. B

In the statement 上网 matches with 电脑 in choice B.

42. D

In the statement, the key words 看看, 新闻, 体育比赛 are related to 看 and 电视节目. So D is the correct answer.

43. C

什么时候 determines that a time expression is needed to answer the question. Among the choices, C 夏天 can be used to answer it.

44. F

This proverb is a little difficult, but 借 and 还 show that this proverb is related to borrowing things. The beginning parts of A and F seem to be feasible, but if we look at their latter parts, we will find 到 in choice A is irrelevant to 借, and yet 用 in choice F is the inevitable result of 借, because you will definitely use whatever you borrow.

45. A

Although we can choose answer A directly as it is the only option left, the choice can still be tested by looking for related words. For example, 坐坐 is related to 到, and 马上到 is the direct reason why the speaker won't rest right away in spite of 腿疼.

Keys to Questions 46—50: E D C B A

46. E

见马经理 shows its reply should be relevant to a person, to which C and E are related. Choice C shows a history lesson will be given, which has nothing to do with 经理, so C should be ruled out leaving E as the correct answer.

47. D

When it comes to changes in a city, urban elements such as streets and houses are often touched upon. In choice D, the houses have been changed into high-rises, which is in line with the changing urban features, so D is the correct answer.

48. C

老师 is mentioned in the statement. 学生 in choice C matches with the statement, so C is the correct answer.

49. B

有多远 should be answered with miles or by the time length of your trip. In choice B, 40 多分钟 is mentioned. So B is the correct answer.

50. A

The statement mentions weather, which often connects with cold and warmth, or sunny and rainy days. In choice A, a cold winter is mentioned; A is the correct answer.

第二部分 Part Two

Keys to Questions 51—55: B A C F D

Tips: To solve this kind of questions students can first use the process of elimination to rule out unrelated choices and then analyze the rest.

51. B

The brackets are followed by 哪儿 in 哪儿有卖报纸的, from which we can deduce that the question is about asking for a location and the related vocabulary. Among the choices, 附近 fits in this context. B is the correct answer.

52. A

The brackets are followed by the character 里, from which we can deduce that a noun indicating a certain scope is needed in this context. 班 is the only suitable choice that functions with the

1

statement 他儿子在他班里最高. So A is the correct answer.

53. C

回答 is easily collocated with 问题. Therefore, C is the correct answer.

54. F

The verb 祝 and the adverb 经常 which indicate frequency are the two options left for this question. And from 带 following the brackets we can deduce that no more verbs are needed in this context. So F 经常 is the correct answer.

55. D

From the wishes 身体健康, 天天快乐, and other ones like 新年快乐 and 生日快乐 we know that the verb 祝 is needed in the context. So D is the correct answer.

Keys to Questions 56—60: B A F E C

Tips: What makes this part more difficult than the last five questions is that set phrases are no longer enough to solve these problems, so students need to take into account the differences regarding parts of speech.

56. B

The brackets are between 我 and 自己, from which we can deduce that a verb is needed to link the subject 我 and the object 自己. Among the choices B and E are verbs, but E 检查 does not fit in this context as it has little to do with expectations for the future. So B 相信 is the correct answer.

57. A

From the flexible date 7 号 we can deduce that 不一定, which indicates uncertainty, is needed at the beginning of the sentence. Although we also have the collocation 不久, it does not fit in this context as the fixed date of return is already mentioned in the statement, which has little to do with time span. So A is the correct answer.

58. F

The two words 蛋糕 and 礼物 come to mind as we see 生日. So F 礼物 is the correct answer.

59. E

Common classroom expressions are tested in this question. After students finish their 作业, the teacher often asks them to 检查 it for possible mistakes. And then the teacher may 检查 the students' 作业 again. 检查 is easily collocated with 作业. So E is the correct answer.

60. C

C 久 is the last option for this question, which has the same meaning as 很长时间.

第三部分　Part Three

61. C

We can find that the first sentence 环境还可以 is the key to the exercise, which is further explained in the following part. The near synonyms 还可以 and 不错 are also tested in this question, thus we can see C corresponds with the first sentence. So A and B can be eliminated.

62. A

B can be eliminated first because based on our common knowledge, as very few characters are contained in a Chinese name. Students maybe misled by C, but the number of characters in 名字 is not mentioned in the question. Instead, the statement is all about 姓. So A is the correct answer.

63. C

米 is not mentioned in the statement, so B can be eliminated. 面 appears once, but it is different from 面条儿. So C is the correct answer which is also the last option.

64. B

春天到了 appears at the end of the statement, so it can be easily deduced that 现在是春季. So B is the correct answer.

65. C

A can be eliminated first as 哭 is not mentioned. We can also eliminate B 总是迟到 because we know of his devotion to his job. From the context we can deduce that he has begun to work. So C is the correct answer.

66. A

下课 in the exercise will be enough to solve this question because students are always expecting this phrase from their 老师.

67. C

去医院 is mentioned at the end of the question, so B can be eliminated first. One may go to the hospital when they catch a cold, but the person's problem is a toothache instead of a headache. So A is not the correct answer.

68. B

In the 虽然 … 但是 structure, the clause led by 但是 is usually the key and should be closely monitored. 会找时间去锻炼身体 indicates that the person often exercises, and the latter part only introduces the sports he is involved with.

69. A

We can deduce from the first sentence 她决定和男朋友结婚了 that A is the correct answer.

70. A

We can deduce from the last sentence that the fish at this restaurant is very delicious. So A is the correct answer. As for the other two choices, mutton is not mentioned, while dishes are just described as not many but not whether the ingredients are fresh or not.

三、写作 Writing Section

第一部分　Part One

71. 这种蛋糕太甜了。

The HSK Level 1 vocabulary 太 and 了 can be used in the 什么 + 太 + adj.+ 了 structure which indicates a high degree. 甜 is the only adjective that fits in this context, and the word that matches 这种 is 蛋糕; hence the complete form, 这个 + 蛋糕 + 太 + 甜 + 了.

72. 这个月花了一万多块钱。

花 and 了 appear together as a phrase in this context which reduces the difficulty of the question, because otherwise students may come up with 这个月花一万多块钱了. Also, 钱 and 块 are not divided which avoids the possibility of 这个月花了钱一万多块. In Chinese, 了 usually follows the verb immediately to indicate something that has already occurred and 块钱 cannot be separated when following an amount of money.

73. 帮助别人是一件快乐的事情。

什么 + 是一（个 / 件）+ 什么 is a commonly used structure; based on this, students may come up with 一件快乐的事情是帮助别人 which is not correct. The reason is that there are a lot of things that can make you feel happy, helping others is just one of them. If the subject and predicate are interchanged, the sentence will become illogical. Moreover, the modifier 一件 together with what is modified cannot appear as the subject.

74. 会议还没有结束呢。

The usage of 还 is tested in this question. When indicating a continuous action or state, 还 should be immediately followed by words such as 在 or 没. So 还没有结束 is the correct collocation, rather than 还结束没有.

75. 她的汉语水平提高得很快。

The knowledge of the difference among 的, 地 and 得 is tested in this question. In this context, the complement 得 is used to link the verb and adjective. Hence with the verb 提高 and adjective 快, the collocation 提高得很快 is formed.

第二部分　Part Two

76. 中

It can be easily deduced from the pinyin and the character 国 that the word should be 中国. This commonly used word is not difficult for students as it is one of the first vocabulary words learned. Note that the 口 part in 中 should be written in separate strokes and the vertical line should be centered.

77. 元

From the decimal relation between 分 and 角 we can deduce that 元, the biggest monetary unit of Chinese currency fits in this context. Note that the upper horizontal line in 元 should be written a bit shorter than the lower one, and the last stroke should be a 乚, not a right falling stroke.

78. 只

From the pinyin we can deduce that 只, which indicates a certain range, fits in this context. The character is not hard to write, but note that the last two strokes should be two dots pointing to the left and right, respectively.

79. 门

The pictographic character 门 is also a radical which is enclosed in three directions. Remember to neither write the dot outside nor inside of the frame. Some messaging software may render this character as 冂, which is not correct.

80. 好

好 can be seen as an associative compound consisting of 女 and 子. The character was originally written as , which symbolizes a mother holding her baby. It represents the idea that becoming a mother is, in and of itself, endowed with goodness.

H31222卷答案解析

一、听力 Listening Section

第一部分 Part One

Keys to Questions 1—5: C B F A E

1. C

In the recording, the word 想 and the man's answer 想这次文化节在哪儿 … correspond with the picture containing a man who is thinking, so C is the correct answer.

2. B

In the recording 吃 is mentioned, which is naturally associated with food. Bread and other foods in Picture B are talked about in the recording, so B is the correct answer.

3. F

In the recording, 搬这么多东西 is mentioned. Although the sense of 开门 isn't embodied in any picture, we can deduce F is the correct answer as it contains boxed items that are being moved.

4. A

In the recording, 这双鞋 is mentioned, which shows that this question is related to buying shoes. Among the pictures, A is correct because it shows a woman trying on shoes.

5. E

After hearing the word 狗, you can easily see that the answer is E.

Keys to Questions 6—10: E D A C B

6. E

After catching the words 作业 and 选择题 in the recording, you can deduce that it is related to studying. If you look at the pictures, you will find Picture E shows two people in a classroom, so E is the correct answer.

7. D

The words 下雨 and 伞 in the recording can help us deduce Picture D is correct because it shows a man holds an umbrella.

8. A

If you hear the words 果汁 and 喝 you will find only Picture A, which shows a lady holding a cup, is related to 喝.

9. C

It is not easy to find the correct answer to this exercise because the key word 画 is mentioned only once. If you are not familiar with the scene mentioned in the recording, it isn't easy to find the answer. However, among the remaining two options, Picture B shows a person climbing stairs, which is unrelated to the topic of the dialogue, so B can be ruled out and C can be confirmed as the correct answer.

10. B

走楼梯 and 电梯 are mentioned in the recording and remind us of climbing stairs as shown in Picture B.

第二部分　Part Two

11. ✓

The last sentence 你还是认真地想想 in the recording means the same as the statement, which demonstrates that the speaker hopes he takes the issue seriously.

12. ✓

A lot of information is mentioned in the recording, such as the lack of bowl and chopsticks for one guest, as well as the intention of ordering more dishes, so the statement fits in with the recording.

13. ×

The condition 会议一结束 expressed in the recording is confusing. If you don't hear it clearly, you will construe it as the conclusion of the meeting. But listening again and you will find the first sentence explicitly states that 正在开会, so this statement is false.

14. ✓

This exercise tests knowledge of synonyms. 他家在公园附近 in the statement is the same as 我们家旁边有个公园 in the recording in terms of meaning, as 附近 and 旁边 are synonyms.

15. ×

You may make a mistake if you only catch several key words, because in the recording the word 北京 is mentioned, but Beijing here actually refers to the city which the guests come from rather than the city which Xiao Gao will go to.

16. ✓

The exercise tests you how to use an antonym to express the same meaning. 离这儿很近 in the recording expresses the same meaning as 离这儿不远 in the statement, so this statement is correct.

17. ✓

In the statement 终于 is a new vocabulary word introduced to explain a goal which can only be achieved through hard work. In the recording it is shown how the speaker eventually comes to comprehend those new words through the help of the teacher. So the statement accords with the recording.

18. ×

This exercise may be easy to get wrong as it is seemingly very simple, so attention should be paid to all of the information available. His brother was a teacher not a student from a middle school. It is not hard to find the answer but easy to miss the key information.

19. ×

The sentence pattern 除了 … 还 used in the recording, which serves to list options, shows there are multiple functions for mobile phones. The statement and the recording are contrary in meaning.

20. ×

This exercise tests the students' arithmetic ability. In the recording, 这个季节 refers to 现在, and the current price is 一公斤要十几块钱. In the statement, 一斤西瓜 won't be likely to cost 一元钱, as 一斤 is half a kilogram.

第三部分　Part Three

21. B

The key to this exercise is to hear 还是你聪明 when the man compliments the woman in the recording. This shows that the man thinks the method put forward by the woman is a good one and she is clever, so B is the correct answer.

22. A

The three choices show the speakers are on the move. In most cases, 慢点儿 and 注意 won't be involved in 跑步, so B should be ruled out. As for the other choices, 开车 and 骑自行车, you will find A is the correct answer because the verb 开 is mentioned in the recording.

23. B

明天 is mentioned first in the dialogue, but is rejected immediately. 周末 is mentioned twice, as well as on the weekend 天气好, as the reason for going, so B is the correct answer.

24. A

The relationship between the different times mentioned by the man and by the woman should be first clarified. The man says he wants to buy a ticket for June 1st while the woman says the tickets before June 2nd are sold out. Since June 1st is before June 2nd, it can be deduced that the tickets on June 1st must be sold out, so A is the correct answer.

25. A

The man mentions that the reason why he eats at night after dinner is that he 没吃饱 and 饿了.

26. C

This is a common sense based exercise. The man asks why she didn't come to work and the woman answers 儿子发烧了. The reason is very common and persuasive, so C is the correct answer while the other two aren't.

27. A

Common knowledge is needed to finish this exercise. In the recording, the word 裤子 in the first sentence 先生, 这是您的裤子 shows the speakers may be in the store since in other scenes it is not likely to talk about trousers in this way. In particular, 欢迎下次再来 is a typical expression used in stores, so A is the correct answer.

28. C

The answer to this exercise is shown indirectly. It should be made clear that the woman's appearance changes compared with the previous photo. She used to be thin, but now she is heavier. In the past, she had long hair, but now her hair is short. Among the choices, 变化不大 in B can't be the answer while 爱照相 in A has nothing to do with the recording. Therefore, C is the correct answer.

29. C

This exercise tests knowledge of synonyms. The sentences 环境不错 and 环境好 have the same meaning. So C is the correct answer; the other two choices aren't mentioned in the recording at all.

30. C

A commonly used abbreviation, 邮件, short for 电子邮件, is employed in the recording.

马上就写完邮件了 mentioned by the man indicates that he 正在写电子邮件.

第四部分　Part Four

31. A

唱歌 is never mentioned in the recording, so choice B can be ruled out. The other two choices are related to ball games, but we need to listen again to decide which one is truly correct. In the recording 打篮球 is mentioned, which can be abbreviated as 打球, so A is the correct answer; choice C 踢足球 should be ruled out.

32. B

Pay attention to where the woman is currently. In the recording, she says she is at 公园门口 and will wait for the man here. Therefore, B is the correct answer as both speakers will meet at the 公园.

33. C

It is easy to find the answer to the exercise by ruling out the least possible choices. The dialogue, centering around a person, has nothing to do with 没吃药 in choice A, as well as 写错字了 in choice B. Only choice C is relevant to the person, so the answer can basically be confirmed. Listening to the recording again, you will find that the man thinks the woman they are talking about is surnamed 马, but her surname is actually 万, which shows that the man has mistaken the woman for someone else.

34. C

It is a little hard to understand the overtone involved in the recording. When the woman says 哪天我们去吃吧, she doesn't intend to ask which day they will go there for dinner, but proposes that they dine there some day. Then the man answers by using the rhetorical question 或者我们现在就去 which shows the man wants to dine there now. So C is the correct answer.

35. C

Ruling out the least possible answers should be employed in the exercise. In the recording, the man first mentions his blue shirt, so B is definitely incorrect. The man and the woman are discussing whether the shirt has been washed, which has no link with whether the shirt is new or old, so A can be ruled out. C can then be confirmed as the correct answer as it is the focus of the recording.

36. B

In the recording, both speakers are talking about a 包 and a 电脑 and never mention 在写

信, so choice A can be ruled out. The woman says she bought a bag online but hasn't received it, so she wants to track it online. This tells us that the woman 想用电脑. Since the woman hasn't received the bag yet, we don't know if she is satisfied with her purchase.

37. B

Ruling out the least possible answers can be used in this exercise. The woman never mentions 腿疼 and 照相机 in the recording, so choice A and C can be ruled out straightaway. 把帽子忘在洗手间了 in the recording is the same as 忘拿帽子了 in terms of their meaning, so B is the correct answer.

38. A

The man says the book is 很有意思, so we know the book is 很不错, which tells us A is the correct answer. In choice C, 中间写得好 can indicate the book is also 很不错, but this choice is inconsistent with the recording; after listening to the recording again you will find the best part of the book has not been mentioned despite the fact that we know the man has finished reading the book from the statement 我一天就把它读完了.

39. B

In the recording, two key points are mentioned by the man: he will take a day off and see the woman off, which has nothing to do with passports. It hasn't been mentioned whether or not the man will be happy when the woman leaves, so B is the correct answer.

40. B

Ruling out the least possible answers can be used in the exercise. 跳舞 isn't mentioned in the recording, so C can be ruled out. 复习 isn't mentioned either when the man talks about the reason why he doesn't attend the competition, so A can be ruled out. 没兴趣 is the real reason and is mentioned twice.

二、阅读 Reading Section

第一部分 Part One

Keys to Questions 41—45: B C D F A

Tips: While doing this type of matching exercise, the key is to find the appropriate words or phrases through the similarities, relevance or connections. The exercises here are designed based on starting from the easiest and moving to the hardest.

41. B

The key to this exercise is to find the antonym of 回 in this context, which is 去, and the question word 怎么 used to ask about conditions, such as 不舒服 as mentioned here.

42. C

In the statement, the speaker would like something to drink since it's hot. The verb 喝 is the key word here. Beverage names are related to the verb 喝, so C can be confirmed as the correct answer which contains such beverages as 咖啡, 果汁, 啤酒.

43. D

In the statement, 裙子 can be matched with 穿. Looking over the choices, only D can be confirmed as the correct answer which contains the action 穿.

44. F

In the statement, the word 找到了 is related to 发现 in the matching answer. Among the two choices left, only F contains the related word 发现.

45. A

看电视 is related to 节目, so A, the last option, is the correct answer.

Keys to Questions 46—50: B E D A C

Tips: The key to this type of exercises is to look for the fixed collocation between nouns and verbs. It is advisable to start with the exercise you find easiest and later move to the hardest.

46. B

We can find the correct answer B after ruling out the other choices. By reading carefully, we find this choice is appropriate because we need to change clothes before going out to buy a dictionary.

47. E

You would think of 礼物 at the sight of the greeting 生日快乐, so E is the correct answer which contains the word 礼物.

48. D

This statement shows a scene when people meet for the first time and are introduced to each other. Since choice D contains the key word 见面, D is the correct answer.

49. A

The opposite meaning of the phrase 空调关了 is 还是开着. The air-conditioner is still on, so A is the correct answer.

50. C

糖 in the statement would make you think of 甜, so it is easy to find that the correct answer is C.

第二部分　Part Two

Keys to Questions 51—55: C　A　B　F　D

51. C

会 preceding the brackets shows a verb is needed. Meanwhile, in addition, 问题 often collocates with 解决, so C is the correct answer.

52. A

A number before and a noun after the brackets indicate that a measure word is needed. Among these choices, only 种 in choice A is a measure word, so A is the correct answer.

53. B

The logic of the statement moves as follows: when it rains, it will become cold, so more clothing should be worn to stop ourselves from catching a cold. Based on this, B is the correct answer.

54. F

The two choices left are nouns. In the statement, we associate 家 with the concepts such as family, neighbor, etc. Choice F represents a neighbor, so F is the correct answer.

55. D

The last word is 城市. The latter part of the statement shows that what I like most is Beijing, and Beijing is a city, so D is the correct answer.

Keys to Questions 56—60: E　B　F　C　A

Tips: This group of exercises is more difficult than last group because fixed collocation cannot help us find the answer to the five exercises. Meaning groups and parts of speech should be taken into consideration.

56. E

真 preceding the brackets indicates that an adjective is needed. 葡萄 is the topic of the statement and 甜 in choice E can be used to best describe a grape, so E is the correct answer.

57. B

会 before the brackets shows a verb is needed. The time expression in the latter part of the statement indicates that B 迟到 is the most appropriate answer.

58. F

What is in the brackets offers no obvious clues to finish this exercise. Without adding any content in the brackets, the statement 这次的题简单 is complete. To fill in the brackets in the sentence, an adverb is needed to modify the adjective following the brackets, so F is the correct answer.

59. C

能 before the brackets indicates that a verb is needed. There is only one verb left, 帮忙, which is in choice C.

60. A

The last choice, A 银行, can collocate with 中国, and these two words 中国 and 银行 can be combined to form the name of a bank which serves as an object here.

第三部分　Part Three

61. B

After browsing the statement, you can directly choose the answer B based on 要看他怎么做 at the end. In case of negligence, we should check the other choices. 关心 in choice A is too vague while choice C is contrary in meaning to the statement.

62. A

This exercise may be confusing. B should be ruled out first because this choice was never mentioned in the statement. The other two choices share some links though. Choice A 少生气 fits in with the statement. Choice C 忘记过去 seems to be correct, but actually is not, because 过去 is vague, including good and bad past events; the statement only suggests people forget bad past events rather than the whole past. Therefore, A is the correct answer.

63. B

The relationship between 电脑 and 普通话 has never been mentioned, so C should be ruled out first. However, 身体, especially 眼睛, is mentioned, thus A may be believed to be the correct answer, but actually isn't. The mention of 眼睛 should not narrow down the scope of meaning of 对 … 身体 … 影响很大. So B is the correct answer.

64. C

Only rice and noodles are mentioned in the recording, as opposed to mutton, so B should be ruled out first. Choice A misses the point while choice C 习惯吃面条了 is the last sentence of the statement, so choice C is the correct answer.

65. A

This statement is not difficult even though it is a little long. Choices C and B can be ruled out because 音乐 and 老师 are not mentioned. In choice A, 下水 and 敢 appear in the statement, so A is the correct answer.

66. A

If you resort to association, you will think taxi drivers should know all the streets, then you will choose C. But this association will not help you find the correct answer. Neither 新车 nor 街道 are mentioned in the statement, but choice A 经常洗车 fits in with the statement.

67. B

This exercise is aimed at testing your understanding of the key words 很急 and 很重要. If something is 很急 and 很重要, that means it is an urgent task that should be given priority. Only choice B expresses this meaning. Even if the issue is hard to handle or another person's help is needed, these things do not express urgency.

68. A

The statement focuses on discussing why the restaurant is attractive, but choices B and C presents the negative sides of a restaurant, so these choices are not the answers to the exercise. Meanwhile 又好吃又便宜 in the statement shows 菜不贵 at this restaurant.

69. C

In the statement, the last sentence 香蕉是长在树上的 is the same as choice C, so C is the correct answer.

70. C

月亮 is never mentioned in the statement, so A should be ruled out. Kitchen is mentioned in the statement, so 在洗盘子 seems to be the answer. However, the final sentence says his sister is making cake, so B can be ruled out, leaving C as the correct answer.

三、写作 Writing Section

第一部分 Part One

71. 她和男朋友准备明年结婚。

It should be noted that some students may form the sentence 她准备明年结婚和男朋友, which contains Thai grammatical features. 和 as used here is similar to 跟. In Chinese, both parties related to an action should closely precede and follow 和.

72. 那个年轻人工作很努力。

In the exercise, the sentence being composed should follow an S+V structure. Some students may offer the following sentence, 那个年轻人很努力工作, which is incorrect because the particle 地 is needed between the adverbial 努力 and the verb 工作. But 地 is not actually offered in the exercise.

73. 这次出现的问题跟上次相同。

It is not easy to compose this sentence, but we can complete it by focusing on the core of the sentence, and then working outward. The core should be 问题. And what about the problems? 问题相同. Which problems are the same? 问题跟上次的相同, problems from this time is the same as last time. Using these clues, you can compose the sentence. As for the usage of 跟, you can turn to exercise 71. The sentence should be constructed as follows:

问题　相同

问题　跟上次的　相同

这次出现的　问题　跟上次的　相同

74. 运动能使人更健康。

Some students may create a sentence like 运动使人能更健康. However, we should remember the principle that 能 must be put before 把, 被 or 使, so 能把 …, 能被 … and 能使 … are the commonly used sentence patterns.

75. 那本书被他借走了。

It is not difficult to compose a sentence with passive voice included. It is person who borrows books instead of book borrowing person, so 书 should be followed by 被, the real doer 他 should be placed after 被, and 了 should be put at the end to indicate the completion of an action.

第二部分　Part Two

76. 从

The pinyin shows 从 is the correct answer. It should be noted that 从 cannot be written as two 人 side by side with much space between each other. The final stroke of 人 on the left side should be changed from a right falling stroke to a dot.

77. 件

This exercise tests the knowledge of the measure word 件. It should be noted that the character cannot be written as 件 or its left radical be mistaken for 彳.

78. 打

打算 is part of the vocabulary of this level, but you have learned 打 as an HSK vocabulary of Level One, as in 打电话. It should be noted that 丁 cannot be written like 十, or vertical hook like vertical rising stroke.

79. 长

长 is a character with more than one pronunciation. If it is used as an adjective, its pronunciation is cháng. When writing this character, you should note that the left-falling stroke in the upper right part cannot be written as a horizontal stroke.

80. 女

It is not difficult to write the character 女 as this character has appeared since we learned the word 你好. It should also be noted that the horizontal stroke in 女 isn't written close to the bottom of the character.

H31223 卷答案解析

一、听力 Listening Section

第一部分　Part One

Keys to Questions 1—5: C　E　B　A　F

Tips: First, quickly look over the pictures and familiarize yourself with the topics. Then think of relevant phrases. After that, begin listening to the recording.

1. C

An item collocating with the measure word 条 and its color are mentioned in the recording, so it can be deduced that the item here refers to a pair of trousers; C is the correct answer.

2. E

The word 新闻 is mentioned in the recording, and it is often presented in a newspaper or on TV. In Picture E, a lady is reading a newspaper. So E is the correct answer.

3

3. B

The key word in the recording is 跑步. In Picture B, two people are running together. So B is the correct answer.

4. A

The word 行李 indicates the answer; only Picture A contains a piece of luggage.

5. F

The word 菜单 appears in the recording, which is reminiscent of people ordering in a restaurant. So F is the correct answer.

Keys to Questions 6—10: B　A　E　C　D

6. B

Two key words, 牙 and 疼, appear in the recording. In Picture B, there is a lady who is suffering from a toothache. So B is the correct answer.

7. A

The correct answer can be deduced after hearing 打扫, because only Picture A contains a man with a mop. The correct answer here is A.

8. E

The word 不太懂 and the request 你再给我讲讲 need to be heard. These will help you to get the sense that two people are discussing a problem. In Picture E, two people are working in front of a computer together, this image fits in with the recording.

9. C

The woman in the recording says she cannot find her 护照, although she remembered she 放在包里了. In Picture C, a lady is fumbling in her bag. This image fits in with the recording. So C is the correct answer.

10. D

In Picture D, things are being moved, which may be related to 搬家. In the recording, the topic of moving house is mentioned. So D is the correct answer.

第二部分 Part Two

11. ✓

The recording focuses on 夏阿姨 and 她很爱笑. 也很热情 is mentioned, too. So the statement is true.

12. ✓

The sentence 一起去游泳 should be focused on in the recording, because it shows the man would like to swim even though he has no time now. The statement is 他打算去游泳, so it is true.

13. ×

In the recording, the speaker says 每天骑自行车去上班, but the statement is 坐公共汽车去上班. They are contrary in meaning, so the statement is false.

14. ×

Attention should be paid to the numbers here. The recording mentions Xiao Li is one year older, and further explains that one was born in December and the other born in January the following year. It means that Xiao Li is just one month older. The statement is 差两岁, which is false.

15. ✓

The key sentence pattern in the recording is 除了 ... 都. This sentence pattern is used to introduce the special circumstance that 马明没有来考试 although all the others have taken exams, so the recording accords with the statement.

16. ×

跳舞是姐姐的爱好 is mentioned at the beginning of the recording, which shows that the sister likes dancing. But the statement is 姐姐喜欢唱歌, so it is false.

17. ×

In the statement, 这个季节 … 特别热 indicates that it's currently summer now, not winter, so the statement is false.

18. ×

A logical relation in the recording 数学学得好的人不一定都是非常聪明的人 should be clarified as follows: Not all people that are good at math are intelligent. What's more important is 有兴趣 and 很努力. The statement cannot convey the meaning of the recording completely, so it is false.

19. ✓

In the recording, 如果长时间放在一起, 香蕉会容易变坏 shows that 香蕉和苹果不要长时间放在一起, so the statement is true.

20. ✓

In the recording, the sentence 早点睡吧 shows 爸爸还没有睡觉, but he is asked to sleep soon, so the statement is true.

第三部分　Part Three

21. A

The key to the recording is that the woman thinks the hotel is 很安静 while the man thinks it is 很方便; it can then be found that choice B 很漂亮 and choice C 很干净 are never mentioned. So A is the correct answer.

22. C

Choice B is ruled out first because marriage is never mentioned in the recording. The sentence 让我明天去上班 shows that the man hasn't gone to work, so it is impossible to deduce whether he is 很忙, then choice A should be ruled out. C is the correct answer.

23. B

The dialogue is an easy one. 房子 has nothing to do with weight, so choice A should be ruled out. 年 instead of people is mentioned, so choice C should be ruled out leaving B as the correct answer.

24. A

The key word in the recording is 旅游, which indicates the correct answer is A.

25. B

The man says the program he wants to watch is 动物世界, so B is the correct answer.

26. C

The woman reminds the man 别一直看电脑, which means 少看电脑. So C is the correct answer.

27. A

The key word in the recording is 王经理, which indicates the correct answer is A.

28. B

It would be difficult to hold a conversation under the circumstances of all the choices, but after hearing the recording, you will find the situation described here is 在开车. So B is the correct answer.

29. A

The expression 等你过去照相 means the woman asks the man to 照相 rather than 买相机. So A is the correct answer.

30. B

The words 咖啡店 and 咖啡 are mentioned once in the recording, so it can be deduced that B is the correct answer.

第四部分　Part Four

31. B

In the recording, the woman says the movie is 很好看 and 很有意思, so B is the correct answer; the other two choices are contrary to the recording in meaning.

32. B

After hearing 你下星期就回国, the time range can be confined within the next week; then the man continues to say 下个周日, so B is the correct answer.

33. C

In the recording, when the man asks the woman if she 感冒了, the woman says she doesn't know. But her description about her physical condition of 累 and 头疼 indicates that she 生病了, so C is the correct answer.

34. A

In the recording, the woman asks 怎么走, which indicates that they are looking for directions, so choice B can be ruled out as it says 灯坏了. The dialogue focuses on looking for directions, but never mentions whether the speakers are agreeing with each other, so C should be ruled out. Actually the man knows the way, so he tells the woman not to worry about getting lost. So A is the correct answer.

35. C

The key to understanding the recording is to catch the phrase 篮球比赛 in the sentence 学校要举行篮球比赛. Based on the recording, it can be deduced that the reason for his daily exercise is 要比赛了. So A is the correct answer.

36. B

We should be clear on a character in the recording, 女儿. Because 女儿上学没带伞 and it is going to rain soon, the man has to 接她, which shows B is the correct answer.

37. C

In the recording, nothing mentioned is related to choice A or B, but choice C describes the key content that the woman 忘带手机了.

3

38. C

In the recording, 我已经进电梯了 demonstrates that the man is currently in the lift. So C 电梯里 is the correct answer.

39. B

再多放点糖 should be the focus of the recording. This shows the man feels that the bread is 不太甜 as he thinks more sugar will be better. So B is the correct answer.

40. A

This recording may be confusing. 同事, 老师, or 学生? From the recording, it can be deduced the person the man encountered is a teacher and a colleague of the man. 同学 and 朋友 are not mentioned in the recording, so A is the correct answer.

二、阅读 Reading Section

第一部分 Part One

Keys to Questions 41—45: C D F B A

Tips: While doing this type of matching exercise, the key is to find the appropriate words or phrases through the similarities, relevance or connections. The exercises here are designed based on starting from the easiest and moving to the hardest.

41. C

Noses and eyes are sensory organs, which are related in appearance between the father and his child mentioned in choice C. So C is the correct answer.

42. D

The verbs 洗 and 穿 are mentioned in the statement and it is associated with clothes. 衬衫 appears in choice D, so this choice matches with this statement.

43. F

服务员 and 少一双筷子 in the statement demonstrate that it is related to dining in a restaurant as well as the number of diners. The number of people is mentioned in choice F, so F is the correct answer.

44. B

借 is linked with 还. 还 is mentioned in choice B. So B is correct.

45. A

汉语水平提高 indicates the improvement of language skills, and 说得越来越好 shows that the man speaks Chinese better and better. So A is the correct answer.

Keys to Questions 46—50: E D B A C

Tips: The key to this type of test questions is to look for the fixed collocation between nouns and verbs. It is advisable to start with the exercise you find easiest and later move to the hardest.

46. E

After going over all of the answers it can be seen that E is correct because after wearing out your glasses you would go to a store to buy a new pair.

47. D

去图书馆 is mentioned in the statement. It shares some links with 查字典 in choice A, 明天考试 in choice C and 学习环境比较好 in choice D. In choice C you will find 关老师说, but generally speaking there won't be classes in the library, therefore, choice C can be ruled out. In choice A, there is the sentence 我也不知道, which is irrelevant to the statement, so choice A should be ruled out, leaving D as the correct answer.

3

48. B

In the statement, the change from 晴天 to 阴天 connects with the weather. 要下雨 appears in choice B, so B is the correct answer.

49. A

A new character is encountered, which is associated with 查词典 in choice A. So A is the correct answer.

50. C

In the statement, 回教室 is a notion closely related to studying. In choice C a teacher and an examination are mentioned, so C is the correct answer.

第二部分　Part Two

Keys to Questions 51—55: D　C　F　B　A

51. D

A word related to shopping and prices should be included here based on the 4 and 5分 before and after the brackets, and the commonly used expression in stores 欢迎再来. 元 and 角 are often used with 分. So 角 in choice D is the correct answer.

52. C

完成 after the brackets and 好好休息 in the latter part of the sentence indicate that they have worked for a long time. 终于 in choice C refers to the outcome produced after a long period of time or much effort. So C is the correct answer.

53. F

In the statement, 真 is followed by the brackets, so an adjective is needed here. 可爱 in choice F is most suitable.

54. B

It can be deduced that a location word is needed here from the latter part of the sentence 让哥哥站后面. In choice B, there is a location word. In the statement, 爷爷和奶奶 is preceded by the brackets, so if we choose B, this sentence will fit with the pattern 谁 + 和 + 谁 + 中间. Therefore B is the correct answer.

55. A

There are two pairs of antonyms, and one is 自己 and 别人, the other is 高 and 低. Therefore, 低 in choice A is the correct answer.

Keys to Questions 56—60: C F A E B

Tips: These five exercises are more difficult than the previous five because collocation is not enough to help find the answer; parts of speech must be taken into account here.

56. C

吃 is mentioned twice in the dialogue, and the outcome of eating, 饱, naturally occurs. So C is the correct answer.

57. F

Two objects are mentioned, and one of the speakers cannot decide what to buy for his mother as a gift. Under this circumstance, 或者 should be used to connect the objects to indicate the gift can be either 裙子 or 帽子. So F is the correct answer.

58. A

The brackets in the dialogue are followed by 点儿, which is often used together with a verb. 小心 is the only verb among the choices. Plates and cups are very fragile, so we should be more careful. Meanwhile, 小心点儿 is a commonly used expression. So A is the correct answer.

59. E

两种 is followed by the brackets, which indicates a noun is needed to collocate with 两种. Among the choices, 办法 is a noun and is linked with 解决问题 mentioned in the latter part of the dialogue. So E is the correct answer.

60. B

敢, or its opposite, 不敢, is used as an auxiliary verb before verbs. So B is the correct answer, which is also the last option.

第三部分 Part Three

61. A

Two time points, 那时 and 现在 are mentioned. Changes occur as time passes, so choice C 和以前相同, should be ruled out. Choice B seems to be correct, but actually isn't because the statement only mentions trees instead of grass. So A is the correct answer.

62. C

Choice B can be ruled out first, because the statement shows the speaker cares for others, not vice versa, and reminds the others to take their belongings. Choice A seems to be correct, but it is not the speaker's main point. What the speaker expects is 别忘记带东西. So C is the correct answer.

63. A

Choice C should be ruled out because second-hand items are still very useful based on common sense. Choice B is incorrect because the statement only introduces the second-hand item, but doesn't mention it is hard to purchase. However, choice A is the same as the sentence "二手"的东西比较便宜 in the statement, so A is the correct answer.

64. C

This statement will mislead you into believing that the garden is very big because a variety of flowers are mentioned in the latter part. The first sentence 我家附近有个花园 is the key point. Although a lot of flowers are mentioned in the statement, this cannot prove the garden is big, let alone that there are many birds in the garden. So C is the correct answer.

65. B

The speaker has worn the shoes mentioned in the statement, which is 非常舒服. It can be deduced that the shoes weren't sold out. The specific color of the shoes, red or another color, isn't mentioned at all. Based on these, A and C should be ruled out and B can be confirmed as the only correct answer.

66. C

It is easy to find the correct answer by ruling out the least possible ones. In the statement, looking at photos is mentioned, but being fearful of dogs and the little sister liking to cry is not. So C is the correct answer which is in line with the statement 她那时很矮.

67. C

The final sentence in the statement 就像在自己家一样 shows that Xiao Yuan is not at home. So C is the correct answer which shows Xiao Yuan 在别人家做客.

68. B

What the teacher says shows no possibilities of 介绍自己 or 回答问题, but the teacher mentions dictation and expects the students to 记得复习 after going home, so B is the correct answer.

69. A

The final sentence 有很多机会 indicates that A is the correct answer.

70. A

The first sentence shows that the speaker 在找东西, which is confirmed by 我必须找到它. The following part is the reason why the lost item must be found, and the clues to help him to find it. So A is the correct answer.

三、写作 Writing Section

第一部分 Part One

71. 睡觉前刷牙是好习惯。

什么是什么 is a classic sentence pattern used to refer to categorization. There is a clear relationship between 睡觉前刷牙 and 好习惯, since 睡觉前刷牙 is a type of good habit. Words indicating broader scope should be placed after 是 while those of narrower scope before it.

72. 客人对我们的服务很满意。

This set of words reminds us of the typical sentence 我们对学习汉语很感兴趣. By modeling it we can make a new sentence, 客人对我们的服务很满意. It is also acceptable to put 对我们的服务 at the beginning. In the new sentence, 服务 is stressed. If we want to use this sentence pattern, a comma is needed, so this sentence can be rewritten as 对我们的服务, 客人很满意.

73. 我现在画小猫的耳朵 / 现在我画小猫的耳朵。

Subject, verb and object should be clarified first and arranged based on the commonly used sentence structure S+V+O. In the group of words, there is another element, time adverbial 现在, which can be put before the subject 我 to emphasize time, or after 我 but before the verb 画 to emphasize the doer. 现在 can never be put at the end of the sentence; it would be the Chinese language with Thai grammatical features.

74. 冰箱里没有啤酒了。

The elements should be arranged based on the sentence pattern 哪里 / 谁 + 有 / 没有 + 什么 + 了. Luckily, 没有啤酒 is offered as a fixed element, therefore, such sentences with Thai features like 冰箱里啤酒没有了 or 冰箱里没有了啤酒 won't occur. 了 in the sentence is used to compose a sentence to indicate a changing condition rather than the completion of an act.

75. 你了解这个国家的文化吗?

The sentence structure S+V+O is tested here. 吗 indicates the arranged sentence must be interrogative. Luckily, 了解这个 and 国家的 are offered as fixed elements, otherwise such sentences like 你了解文化的国家这个吗? would appear, which is a typical Thai sentence pattern with an attributive post position.

第二部分 Part Two

76. 心

The character 心 in the word 放心 is not difficult to write. Attention should be paid to the

3

reclining hook in the lower part, which should be smooth and round and take on a reclining shape. If it looks like a sloping hook, it will appear awkward.

77. 市

市 in the word 城市 can be used to form the word 超市, an HSK vocabulary word in the same level. Special attention should be paid to the upper dot with the direction from left to right as well as 乛 at the lower end when writing.

78. 出

出 in the word 出现 is the same as 出 in 出租车. The character looks like two 山 on top of each other. Attention should be paid to the vertical stroke in the middle of 出, which is required to be written from the top to the bottom.

79. 生

生 in the word 生日 has appeared in the Level 2 vocabulary word 学生. 生 here means "be born."

80. 下

This character and 上 are typical self-explanatory characters with the opposite meanings. The final stroke of 上 is a horizontal stroke while that of 下 is a dot.

H31224 卷答案解析

一、听力 Listening Section

第一部分 Part One

Keys to Questions 1—5: B A E F C

Tips: First, quickly look over the pictures and familiarize yourself with the topics. Then think of relevant phrases. After that, begin listening to the recording.

1. B

In the recording, 吃 and 西瓜 are mentioned. So B is the correct answer.

2. A

In the recording, 字典 is mentioned, and A is the only answer that contains the picture of a book.

3. E

In the recording, 车 is the key word, and E is the only answer that contains the picture of a car.

4. F

Words like 医生 and 出院 are mentioned in the recording, which leads us to think that the man is in hospital. F is the only answer showing a man lying in bed.

5. C

In the recording, 啤酒 is mentioned. So C is the correct answer which is also the last option.

Keys to Questions 6—10: D C B E A

6. D

We can deduce from 照张照片 that the conversation may relate to "camera," and D is the answer which contains the picture of a camera.

7. C

From the word 爸爸 in the recording we can find the picture that contains a father and his daughter, so C is the correct answer.

8. B

We hear the amount of money in the recording first, and then 我找找. B contains a picture showing someone looking for something, so it is the correct answer.

4

9. E

From 鞋不舒服 and 脚疼 in the recording we can deduce that the conversation may relate to "foot." E contains a picture showing someone sitting and rubbing her foot. So E is the correct answer.

10. A

From 把洗手间的灯关了 in the recording we can relate it to the picture showing the light being switched off. So A is the correct answer.

第二部分　Part Two

11. ✓

From 图书馆很安静 in the recording we can deduce that the study environment there is good. So the statement is true.

12. ✓

From 有时间我介绍你们认识 in the recording we can deduce that he wants to introduce his uncle to Xiao Gao. So the statement is true.

13. ✓

In the recording, 儿子 and 牙疼 are mentioned. We can also deduce that the son is ill from the word 发烧. So the statement is true.

14. ×

According to common knowledge, rivers are usually indicated in blue on a map. The recording also mentions that 蓝色的是河流, which runs counter to the statement 蓝色表示的是树. So the statement is false.

15. ✓

The recording mentions that he 喜欢画画，特别喜欢画小动物, which is in line with 他爱画小动物. So the statement is true.

16. ×

The recording mentions 他脸比我小，鼻子也比我高, which is against 他的鼻子比哥哥的高. So the statement is false.

17. ×

The recording mentions 这是您要的咖啡, which indicates that 那位小姐要了杯牛奶 is not correct. So the statement is false.

4

18. ×

The recording mentions 考试 10 点结束, which is against 考试 10 点开始. So the statement is false.

19. √

The recording mentions 有几个朋友要来玩儿, which indicates that 明天有客人来 is correct. So the statement is true.

20. ×

普通话讲得这么好已经不容易了 in the recording indicates that the person can speak Mandarin very well, which runs counter to the statement 普通话说得一般. So the statement is false.

第三部分　Part Three

21. A

老师 and 同学 are the two key words in the recording that show a conversation between the teacher and students. So A is the correct answer.

22. A

越来越可爱 is the key phrase in the recording which indicates the man thinks Xiaoqing is 很可爱. So A is the correct answer.

23. A

We should understand that 打车 and 坐出租车 share the same meaning. As well, subway and bicycle are not mentioned in the recording. So A is the correct answer.

24. C

The only way to solve this problem is to listen carefully. We should pick 9 月 first in the recording and then figure out the date, which is 6 号. So C is the correct answer.

25. B

The man is making a lot of noise playing games while his younger sister is doing her homework. So the woman tells the man to 把声音关小, but doesn't ask him to 教妹妹 or 复习. So B is the correct answer.

26. C

面条儿 is the key word here because the other two choices are not mentioned in the recording. So C is the correct answer.

27. B

经理 is the key word to solve this problem. So B is the correct answer.

28. A

The first key word in the recording is 买, and the other is 换. These two actions could only occur in a shop. So A is the correct answer.

29. C

参加唱歌比赛 is the key expression in the recording. So C is the correct answer.

30. B

Students are likely to confuse B with C in this question. But after listening to the recording again, they may find that in 机票还有吗, 机票 is the key information, rather than 接人. So B is the correct answer.

第四部分 Part Four

31. A

Looking for 手表 is mentioned at the beginning of the recording, but then 在裤子里 is provided as a clue, which may lead some students to choose B. Yet students should keep in mind that what the man is looking for is his 手表. So A is the correct answer.

32. C

The whole recording is about selecting 相机, so C is the correct answer.

33. B

The two choices 九点零五 and 九点五十 are pretty close to each other, but the man mentions 九点零五 in the recording, so B is the correct answer.

34. B

The word 后面 is key to solving this problem, which can also be understood as 附近. Some students may choose C only by picking up 后面, which is wrong. Instead, they should pay attention to the key information 公园. B is the correct answer.

35. C

In the recording, the man asks 能不能再快点, which is key to solving this problem. The man wants that the work to be finished sooner, but doesn't express any dissatisfaction. So C is the correct answer.

36. A

The key is to distinguish whether the man's opinion or the woman's is required here. The man thinks the grapes are 不贵, while the woman thinks they are 新鲜. The woman's opinion is asked in this question, so A is the correct answer.

37. A

The recording mentions that the female wants to go to her friend's home and see 茶花, so it can be deduced that the girl will 看花 the day after tomorrow. Therefore B is the correct answer.

38. B

那个高中同学 is mentioned in the conversation between the man and woman, thus we can deduce that B is the correct answer.

39. B

The recording mentions the man 忘记拿眼镜 and wants to sit in the front to see the blackboard. So B is the correct answer.

40. C

The man says 冬天太冷了 at the end of the conversation, which is key to solving this problem as it indicates that he thinks the winter there is very cold. So C is the correct answer.

二、阅读 Reading Section

第一部分 Part One

Keys to Questions 41—45: F C B D A

Tips: While doing this kind of matching exercises, the key is to find the appropriate words or phrases through the similarities, relevance or connections between the two words or phrases. In the meantime, the process of elimination can be employed and we can find the answer to the easiest question first and then the rest will become easier.

41. F

The key to solving this problem is to find a pair of antonyms, 旧 and 新. So F 买个新的 is the correct answer.

42. C

努力 and 成绩 are mentioned in the statement, thus we can associate them with exam or match. C mentions 游泳比赛, so it is the correct answer.

43. B

Words related to travel like 火车 and 累 are mentioned in the statement, thus we can associate them with ticket or luggage. B mentions 行李箱, so it is the correct answer.

44. D

The word 饭馆儿 could make us think of 服务员, 点菜 or 碗筷, which are all included in D. So D is the correct answer.

45. A

Students should think of 解决问题 as soon as they see the word 办法, which corresponds with A. So A is the correct answer.

Keys to Questions 46—50: C B E D A

Tips: Students should stick to the association method along with the assistance of the elimination method.

46. C

The word 照相 can make us think of 笑 or counting numbers. C mentions 来笑一笑，一二三，so it is the correct answer.

47. B

The phrase 坐电梯 could make many people think of stairways, floors or going up and down stairs. B mentions that the cinema is on 四层, and they are going to 走上去. So B is the correct answer.

48. E

The two pairs of antonyms 睡觉 and 起床, 不饿 and 吃早饭 could provide clues to us, and all of them can be found in E, which is the correct answer.

49. D

From 除了小云，其他人都来了 we can deduce that Xiaoyun has not arrived yet. Thus we should look for words related to 来 or 到, which can be found in 马上就到 in D. So D is the correct answer.

50. A

借我看看 indicates that the person wants to borrow a book, which corresponds with A. So A is the correct answer.

第二部分　Part Two

Keys to Questions 51—55: F B C A D

Tips: Students should pay more attention to parts of speech and set phrases.

51. F

The brackets are followed by 这样的事儿, so a verb is needed in this context. 打扫 and

遇到 are the two verbs provided, but only 遇到 can form a set phrase with 事儿. So F is the correct answer.

52. B

The verb 听 is followed by the brackets, so we can easily figure out that only 声音 and 音乐 can be used in this context. As E has been used in the example, B is the correct answer.

53. C

Students should think of the word 一共 when seeing the monetary unit 9000 yuan, and among the other two choices left, one is an adjective, the other is a verb, neither of which corresponds with money. So C is the correct answer.

54. A

From 口 and 要不要喝杯水, we can deduce that they relate to the character 渴, which can form the phrase 口渴 with 口. So A is the correct answer.

55. D

A verb that corresponds with room is needed here, 打扫 is such a word which is commonly used. So D is the correct answer.

Keys to Questions 56—60: A B F E C

Tips: What makes this part more difficult than the last five questions is that set phrases are no longer enough to solve these problems, so students need to take into account the differences regarding parts of speech.

56. A

The brackets are followed by 哪儿, so a verb is required in this context. And according to 桌子上, we can deduce that the phrase 放哪儿 is needed here. So A is the correct answer.

57. B

The brackets are preceded by 不太, so an adjective is required in this context. And according to 检查, we can deduce that the adjective 舒服 is needed here because people only have a medical check-up when they don't feel well. So B is the correct answer.

58. F

Expressions like 小心 and 到学校给家打电话 are often used by parents when sending their children to school. The children usually reply to their parents by saying 我会照顾好自己. So F is the correct answer.

59. E

The brackets are preceded by 去, so a noun indicating a place is required in this context. And 厨房 is the place where sugar is most likely to be stored, so E is the correct answer.

60. C

C 以前 is the only choice left for this question, and we can deduce from 去年秋天才搬走的 that the speaker no longer lives here now. So C is the correct answer.

第三部分　Part Three

61. A

We can find the answer by analyzing the sentence 很多动物都有站着睡觉的习惯, which can be split into 很多种动物 and 站着睡觉. So A is the correct answer.

62. B

B mentions 蛋糕很好吃, which corresponds with the statement 蛋糕和面包好吃极了, so it is the correct answer.

63. C

Based on common sense, we know the sun never rises in the west no matter 下雨 or 生气. As a result, the sun rises in the west is 不太可能的事. So C is the correct answer.

64. B

The first sentence in the statement 时间有多么重要 indicates B is the correct answer, which is 时间很重要.

65. A

The statement does not mention 少出门, so B should be eliminated first. Though C mentions "going traveling," it refers to 去北方, not to the south as in the statement. So A is the correct answer.

66. C

A 校长 can be eliminated first as soon as we see 王阿姨是老师, and we can deduce that Aunt Wang is 历史老师 from 教世界历史. So C is the correct answer.

67. B

如果他不相信自己, 很难把事情做好 indicates one should believe in themselves if they want to do something well. So B 相信自己 is the correct answer.

68. C

As an irrelevant choice, A 很矮 can be eliminated first. B mentions brother likes to 打球, which usually refers to playing basketball or other ball games except soccer. And brother loves

4

to watch soccer games is mentioned in the statement, so C is the correct answer.

69. C

We can deduce that C is the correct answer as we read the second sentence 这药要饭前吃.

70. A

The statement mentions several expressions used when bidding farewell to others, such as 希望再来，欢迎来玩儿 and 给我写信，which all indicate that the person 要离开. So A is the correct answer.

三、写作 Writing Section

第一部分 Part One

71. 我还以为表演结束了。

以为 is used to introduce a judgment of something, while 还以为 is often used when the judgment does not conform with the fact. 还以为 is followed by 表演结束了 which serves as the object of the sentence. 了 cannot immediately follow 以为. Instead, it should follow the verb in the object phrase to indicate the tense.

72. 那件衬衫才两百元。

We can apply the grammar rules in the Thai language in this context, and 才 should precede the number when indicating a relatively low degree.

73. 这两个词语意思相同。

The question maybe not that hard for Thai students as both the Thai and Chinese languages contain adjectives used as predicates which can replace certain verbs. So this sentence can be translated according to the word order of the Thai language.

74. 果汁被弟弟喝完了。

This is a passive voice sentence. Firstly, the elements before and after 被 should be set: the element indicating the item should precede 被, and the one indicating the person should follow. In the end, the verb and 了 are added to form the complete sentence.

75. 了解历史是为了更好地了解现在。

In a 是 sentence that contains two coordinate clauses, two similar structures are usually placed before and after 是, respectively. For example, before 是 is the four-character phrase 了解历史, thus we should form another four-character phrase 了解现在 and put it after 是. 为了 which introduces the aim of 了解现在 should appear between 是 and 了解现在. So we can get 了解历史 + 是 + 为了 + 了解现在.

第二部分 Part Two

76. 几

几 is one of the few homophones which can be found in both the Chinese and Thai languages. It is not easy to write the character 几 well even though it only contains two strokes. Don't write it like the frame of 风, nor write it like 九.

77. 把

把 is a typical pictophonetic character. Characters like 爸 and 吧 which contain the right-side component of 把 appear frequently in HSK Level 1 and Level 2. We can find that 把 is often associated with actions, and this character contains the radical 扌, which relates to the hands.

78. 忙

Technically speaking, 忙 is one of the vocabulary words in HSK Level 2. Don't write its right component 亡 like 匚.

79. 定

决定 and 一定 are the key vocabulary phrases in HSK Level 3. The lower part of 定 is difficult to write as the character is often presented to students in the Song style typeface, which may lead many people to simply write the bottom part of it as 人.

80. 多

多 is composed of two 夕. It may assist our memorization that "only one 夕 is not enough, another one is needed to form the character 多." Don't write it like 夕夕. Instead, the two 夕 should be placed on a vertical line.

4

H31225 卷答案解析

一、听力 Listening Section

第一部分 Part One

Keys to Questions 1—5: C B A E F

Tips: First, quickly look over the pictures and familiarize yourself with the topics. Then think of relevant phrases. After that, begin listening to the recording.

1. C

In the recording, 葡萄 is mentioned. So C is the correct answer.

2. B

In the recording, 盘子 is mentioned. So C is the correct answer in which a lady is holding some dishes.

3. A

In the recording, 看报纸 is mentioned. So A is the correct answer in which there is a newspaper.

4. E

In the recording, 腿疼 is mentioned. So E is the correct answer in which one person is massaging the other's leg.

5. F

In the recording, the verb 看 and some numbers are mentioned. So the speakers are checking numbers and F is the correct answer.

Keys to Questions 6—10: B C E A D

6. B

In the recording, 头发 and 再长点儿 are mentioned. So B is the correct answer in which a lady is looking at a mirror.

7. C

In the recording, you can hear 看见前面那个车站了吗. So it's about asking directions. C is the correct answer in which one person is signaling direction with his hand.

8. E

In the recording, you can hear 做什么好吃的. It's about food. So E is the correct answer.

9. A

In the recording, two time words 三十分钟 and 十分钟 are mentioned. So A is the correct answer in which a lady is looking at her watch.

10. D

In the recording, you can hear 写作业, so D is the correct answer.

第二部分 Part Two

11. ×

In the recording, the last phrase is 准备睡觉了. The statement is 还没起床. They are contrary in meaning. So the statement is false.

12. ×

In the recording, it is mentioned that after 努力, one's Chinese has gained much improvement. So 没起什么作用 is incorrect. The statement is false.

13. ✓

This exercise is about understanding of synonyms. In the recording, 不远 in 离我家不远有一条小河 is the synonym of 附近 in the statement 他家附近有条小河. So the statement is true.

14. ✓

This exercise is still about understanding of synonyms. In the recording, 不怎么 in 我不怎么喝酒 is the synonym of 很少 in the statement 他很少喝酒. So the statement is true.

15. ×

This exercise is an easy one. When you hear 音乐老师, you can discern that the statement 他是教数学的 is false.

16. ×

In the recording, you can hear 希望姐姐拿到好成绩. Pay attention to 希望 which indicates sister hasn't taken the exam yet. So it's incorrect to say sister 拿了第一名. The statement is false.

17. ✓

If you hear 天气变冷了 in the recording, you will know the statement is true.

18. ×

In the recording, you can hear 南方人多喜欢吃米饭. So the statement 北方人更爱吃米

饭 is false as people in the south prefer rice.

19. ✓

In the recording, the manager asked the speaker 愿不愿意去国外 and the speaker said 同意了. It indicates the speaker 决定去国外, so the statement is true.

20. ✓

In the recording, the last sentence is 小时候的日子是最快乐的 which means the same as the statement 他觉得小时候最快乐. So the statement is true.

第三部分　Part Three

21. C

In the recording, the two key phrases are 需不需要我帮忙 and 不需要, which shows the man is capable of finishing it himself. So C is the correct answer.

22. A

For this exercise, the key point is to know which ball game needs to collocate with the verb 踢. As 踢足球 is a collocation. So A is the correct answer.

23. B

In the recording, the man said 查一下字典 at the end. So B 查字典 is the correct answer.

24. A

In the recording, the man said 我有点儿饿了 at the beginning. So A 饿了 is the correct answer.

25. C

The first sentence in the recording is 这是我第一次下水. The meaning of 下水 and 游泳 are the same. So C is the correct answer.

26. B

In the recording, it is mentioned that 环境很安静 and there is also a 花园, which means the environment is good. So B is the correct answer.

27. A

In the recording, the man mentioned 同学家. So A is the correct answer.

28. B

In the recording, the key messages are that the man asked 你新买的 and the woman answered 是. So B 买新车了 is the correct answer.

5

29. A

In the recording, the man said 我有点发烧, which indicates the man 生病了. So A is the correct answer.

30. C

In the recording, the key message is 黄色, so C is the correct answer.

第四部分　Part Four

31. B

The conversation is about borrowing books. From the conversation, you can tell the man has time to read books. 你还有别的书吗 indicates that 不喜欢看书 is not the correct description for the man. So choice A can be ruled out. The man said the woman lent the books to him and he was returning the book to the woman, which indicates they are not in the library and the man borrowed books from the woman. So choice C can be ruled out. B is the correct answer.

32. A

In the conversation, the verb 搬 appears many times. A common collocation of 搬 is 搬家. Choices B and C have nothing to do with 搬. So A is the correct answer.

33. C

This exercise cannot be done using common senses and therefore requires careful listening. Choices A and B are not mentioned in the recording. 是朋友送的 appears in the conversation. So C is the correct answer.

34. C

In the recording, there is only one time word 下星期五. So clearly C is the correct answer.

35. A

In the recording, the key messages are 灯 and its description 坏了. So A is the correct answer instead of B.

36. A

In the recording, when you hear 太旧了, you can decide A is the correct answer.

37. A

In this exercise, C is the trick answer. Although writing characters is part of learning Chinese, it is more specific. So A 写汉字 is the correct answer.

38. B

The second word in the recording is 秋游 which makes the answer obvious. So the correct answer is B.

39. C

In the recording, the key message is the phrase 西方文化. So C is the correct answer.

40. B

In the recording, the key information is 火车票还有吗. So the means of transportation adopted is 坐火车. B is the correct answer.

二、阅读 Reading Section

第一部分 Part One

Keys to Questions 41—45: D A F C B

Tips: While doing this kind of matching exercises, the key is to find the appropriate words or phrases through the similarities, relevance or connections between the two words or phrases. In the meantime, the process of elimination can be employed and we can find the answer to the easiest question first so the remaining questions are easier to discern.

41. D

The key to connecting the answer to the statement is to find two words of similar meaning: 遇到 and 见面. Another connection 以前的邻居 is more important, which indicates that someone has already 搬走. You can easily find 搬走 in choice D. So D is the correct answer.

42. A

In the statement, 礼物 is mentioned. One can associate 生日 with 礼物. Choice A is about mother's 生日.

43. F

In the statement, there is 喜欢吃. So the answer has something to do with eating, for example, food, kitchen, restaurant and etc. So the correct answer is F which mentions 饭馆儿 and 羊肉.

44. C

From 6 层, one can relate it to elevator, staircase, going upstairs/downstairs and other similar words. Choice C mentions some such words so it is the correct answer.

45. B

From 电子邮件, one can relate it to 电脑 or 手机. Choice B mentions 电脑 so it is the correct answer.

Keys to Questions 46—50: C E A B D

Tips: We can still use association and connection of words to complete this kind of exercises. We can also use the process of elimination. Remember you don't have to start with the first exercise.

46. C

The statement is a description of a woman's physical features—her weight specifically. So the relevant answer is C in which my wife is mentioned. So C is the correct answer.

47. E

冬天 is one of the four seasons. So the answer might be about the seasons. E puts forward the question: which one do you prefer among 四个季节. So E is the correct answer.

48. A

This statement is about going to the zoo and it can be the answer to the question 去哪儿. So answer A 你打算去哪儿玩儿 is the correct answer.

49. B

他正在买衣服 can be associated with 服务员, purchases, clothes and money. Choice B mentions salesperson, pants and exchange of pants, so it is the correct answer.

50. D

Exercise 50 is a question asking 学了多久. So the answer should include 学了 + 时间. Answer D mentions 从七岁开始学, which gives the point of time one began to study (dancing). So D is the correct answer.

第二部分 Part Two

Keys to Questions 51—55: F D C A B

Tips: This part is more difficult than that in the first four exam papers. We can still try to find the answers through excluding incorrect answers and through relevance of meaning. In the meantime we can try other approaches. First, finish simple exercises by going through the answers. For example, 蓝 is a kind of color. So the exercise may also mention other color(s); while 新鲜 often collocates with vegetables and fruits; and 信 often collocates with 写; 努力 often modifies work or study; 站 might have something to do with 坐. So after giving some thought to the answers first, finishing such exercises will become much easier.

51. F

After the brackets comes 想办法解决这个问题. Problem solving is a kind of work. So we can try to put into the brackets 努力—a common collocation of 工作. With 努力, the whole sentence becomes smooth and clearer. So F is the correct answer.

52. D

Before the brackets is the verb 写. 写信 is a collocation so D is the correct answer.

53. C

This statement is also an idiom which may sound difficult. But we can figure out the answer without knowing the idiom. Idioms are often antithetical. 看得远 is antithetical to ( ) 得高. 远 and 高 are both adjectives; so in the brackets, there should be a one-character verb. 站 is the appropriate answer. So C is the correct answer.

54. A

The word in the brackets modifies 天, and after 天, 白 modifies 云 and indicates the color of 云. So A 蓝, a word indicating the color of the sky, is the correct answer.

55. B

A simple approach to answer this question is to immediately associate 水果 with B 新鲜. In terms of language structure, in the construction 又 … 又 …, the words after each 又 should be of the same part of speech and of relevant meaning. The word after the second 又 is 便宜. So in the brackets, there should be a two-character adjective. Therefore 新鲜 is the correct answer.

Keys to Questions 56—60: B A E F C

Tips: This part is easier than the above five exercises. We can figure out the answers through collocations.

56. B

After the brackets is 自行车, so B 骑 is the correct collocation.

57. A

请问您几位 is an expression commonly used in restaurants. So A 菜单 fits the context.

58. E

From 叔叔送 and 不用了, we can infer that the speaker is going to the airport by himself or herself. So E is the correct answer.

59. F

When people lose something, they naturally feel surprised at first. So C 奇怪 is the correct answer.

60. C

The measure word for 裙子 is 条. So C is the correct answer, which is also the last option.

第三部分　Part Three

61. B

Read the exercise and you can find a logical connection: more sugar will result in a sweeter taste. So B is the correct answer.

62. A

This statement introduces what the street was like and what it is like now. It is also mentioned that its present look is different from what it used to be. So A 变化很大 is the correct answer.

63. C

The last sentence in the statement, 别人说的话你没放心上 makes the answer obvious. So C 没放心上 is the correct answer.

64. B

很多东西是书本学不到的 appears at the end of the statement. It indicates that traveling can help him 学到很多. So B is the correct answer.

65. C

The key to this exercise is to know expressions of similar meanings. 相机没带 and 忘记带相机 have the same meaning. So C is the correct answer.

66. B

The second sentence in the statement says 主要介绍中国人的姓. So B is the correct answer.

67. C

The first sentence of the statement makes it clear that the exam is 很容易. So we can infer that the children won't feel 很难过 and they didn't 考得很差. A and B are therefore ruled out. From 讲一个小故事, we can infer that the children 故事讲得不错. So C is the correct answer.

68. A

The key to this exercise is still the understanding of expressions of the same meaning. 身体特别好 means the same as 很健康. So A is the correct answer.

69. C

In the statement, the narrator says 不想这么早结婚 which shows he/she 还不想结婚. So C is the correct answer.

70. B

This exercise can be answered through process of elimination. First of all, 作业 is not mentioned in the statement. So we can exclude A. From 了解他 and 认识他 we can infer it is not about 了解自己. So C 看清楚自己 should be excluded. Therefore, B is the correct answer.

三、写作 Writing Section

第一部分 Part One

71. 祝您节日快乐！

We can use the structure of the expressions 祝你生日快乐 and 祝你新年快乐 to complete this exercise.

72. 你们年级有多少个班？

A common trick answer to this exercise is 你们年纪有班多少个. In Chinese, the question word 多少 should precede the measure word and then the object.

73. 今天终于出太阳了

The key to this exercise is the structure 终于 + verb which indicates a result after a long time.

74. 他不敢把这件事告诉大家。

Follow the structure of 谁 + 把 + 什么 + 怎么样 and identify the sentence components on either side of 把. Then we can find the main part of the sentence 他把这件事告诉大家. 不敢 reflects a state of mind, so 不敢 should follow the person, thus 他不敢. Finally 把这件事告诉大家 follows 他不敢.

75. 哥哥早上习惯喝一杯果汁。

A common collocation is 习惯 + verb. The verb here is 喝. So we can get 习惯喝. Then we add the subject and the object to get the answer 哥哥早上习惯喝一杯果汁.

第二部分 Part Two

76. 是

The key to this exercise is the 是 … 的 structure. 是 is a common character that appears from the beginning of your Chinese learning and throughout the whole process. Pay attention to the bottom part of the character that is not 人. And the top part of 是 is 日 instead of 曰.

5

77. 坐

做 and 作 are also commonly used characters with the pronunciation of zuò. However, the answer to this exercise is a pictographic character. From 坐, you can find two people sitting on the top of a pile of soil. While writing the character, imagine that the pile of soil is rather tall that it separates the two people.

78. 字

字 in 名字 has the top part 宀 and the bottom part 子. Remember not to write 字 incorrectly as 子 or 学.

79. 才

才 indicates a low degree. Don't write the wrong form 扌.

80. 千

千 only has three strokes but there are many characters with similar structures, such as 干 and 于. Pay attention to the first stroke of 千; it's a left falling stroke instead of a horizontal one. The last stroke of 千 is a vertical stroke, not a hook.

策　　划：全球 HSK 策划大队
责任编辑：史文华
英文翻译：张　乐　甄心悦
校　　对：梁　杉

图书在版编目（CIP）数据

HSK 真题集解析 : 2014 版 . 三级 / 孙中华 , (泰) 冯丽颖主编 . — 北京 : 华语教学出版社 , 2014.7

ISBN 978-7-5138-0724-1

Ⅰ . ① H… Ⅱ . ①孙… ②冯… Ⅲ . ①汉语 – 对外汉语教学 – 水平考试 – 题解 Ⅳ . ① H195

中国版本图书馆 CIP 数据核字 (2014) 第 155031 号

HSK 真题集解析（三级）2014 版

孙中华　(泰) 冯丽颖主编

*

华语教学出版社有限责任公司出版
（中国北京百万庄大街 24 号　邮政编码 100037）
电话 : (86)10-68320585, 68997826
传真 : (86)10-68997826, 68326333
网址：www.sinolingua.com.cn
电子信箱：hyjx@sinolingua.com.cn
新浪微博地址：http://weibo.com/sinolinguavip
北京京华虎彩印刷有限公司印刷
2014 年（16 开）第 1 版
2014 年第 1 版第 1 次印刷
ISBN 978-7-5138-0724-1
定价：19.00 元